The Good AND THE Beautiful

MY THIRD
NATURE READER

Written by Jenny Phillips
and Maggie Felsch

Cover illustration by Yana Zybina

goodandbeautiful.com

TABLE OF CONTENTS

BOOK
1

SQUID

QU

The Good and the Beautiful

Illustrated by Rhiannon Archard

© 2022 Jenny Phillips

goodandbeautiful.com

What is this strange, tube-shaped animal with huge eyes and ten squishy arms?

If you said it's a squid, you are right!

A group of squid is called a *squad*!
This squad of squid is on a quest for a
yummy dinner.

Squid are also food for other sea animals at times, so they have at least two tricks to get away.

First, squid can hide quite well in their aquatic homes by changing their color.

Second, squid can squirt an inky liquid into the water and quickly swim away!

Some squid are only about the size of a quarter, while giant squid can grow to the size of a school bus!

BOOK
2

KNOX
ON THE HUNT

KN

The
Good AND THE Beautiful

Knox packs his knapsack with a
camera, a pocketknife, and a snack.
He kneels down and ties his shoes.
He's ready to go on a hunt!

Knox hunts with his camera. He wants more knowledge of the plants and animals around him.

Click! His first picture is of the twisty knots on an ash tree. He does not know how the tree got those knots, but it looks so neat!

Knock, knock, knock, knock!

Knox looks up. What made that sound?
Knox wants to know.

14

There, in an oak tree, an acorn woodpecker is knocking away. Knox does not know why the bird does that, but it is so pretty!

Click!

Knox feels something land on his knuckle. He holds perfectly still. He can take a picture in his mind so he does not scare it away.

OUR CREATOR'S WORLD

BOOK 3

OR Can Say /ER/

The Good AND THE Beautiful

When I see the world
Our Creator made for me,
From the running horse
To the tiny worker bee,
I worship Him.

Sing glory to the Author
Who made it all,
From the worms in the soil
To the colors of fall.

Shout praise to my Anchor
Who made the big trees,
The lakes like glass mirrors,
The stars, and the seas.

So whether I'm having
My worst day or best,
I sit in God's beauty
And in Him find rest.

GREEN ANACONDA

Sight Words: Group 1

Illustrated by Megan Higgins

goodandbeautiful.com

In South America, in a country called Peru,
lives one of the longest snakes in the world.
This is the green anaconda.

The area where she lives has lots of water, for she swims well, and lots of tropical trees and plants.

If she stretched herself into a straight line, she would be as long as five men put together! She will grow up to nine meters (thirty feet) long!

She caught and ate her own breakfast this morning. The lumps in her body could be from any of these animals below. Which do you think she ate?

Now that her belly is full, she doesn't need to eat again for a very long period of time—for weeks or even months!

A group of spider monkeys watches the anaconda safely from the trees. She is beautiful, but they know to stay far away from her.

BOOK
5

GREAT HORNED OWL

Sight Words: Group 1

The Good and the Beautiful

Hoot! Hoot!

Hear that? Deep in the woods, by the trickling brook, is a family of great horned owls. They have no horns at all, just tufts of feathers on their heads.

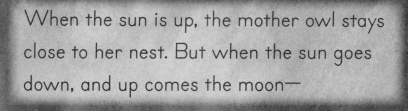

When the sun is up, the mother owl stays close to her nest. But when the sun goes down, and up comes the moon—

she is out and about,
like the masked raccoon.

Looking for food, she flies past flowers in bloom, insects, and a butterfly cocoon.

(Can you find them all?)

Pretty soon, she spots some food. Her family likes to eat mice, rats, squirrels, lizards, smaller birds, snakes, frogs, and more.

With her very good ears and eyes, she swoops down and catches a skunk on her first try—proof that she is a great hunter!

The skunk is much heavier than she is, but she has no trouble carrying it back to her nest in the woods by the brook.

PANDA BEAR

Sounds of OO; Sounds of EAR

Good and the Beautiful

Illustrated by Rhiannon Archard

goodandbeautiful.com

What kind of bear is giant and has large, sharp teeth but appears as dear and sweet as a teddy bear?

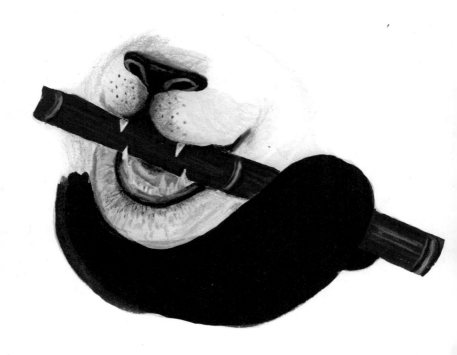

The giant panda bear!

With his pearl-white and pitch-black fur, black spots on his eyes, and cute black ears (that hear very well), the giant panda looks very cuddly.

You do not need to fear him, but just in case, do not get too near.

How would you like to eat the same thing every day, all year? That's what giant panda bears do!

They spend at least ten hours each day
eating bamboo, a type of tall, hard grass.
Their sharp, strong teeth tear it into bits.

Panda bear cubs are born pink and about the size of a pear. They grow fast and learn at an early age—about one and a half to two years old—how to live on their own.

Honey bee, oh, honey bee
Buzzing your cheerful melody,
Zooming around the valley green,
With two pairs of sturdy wings.

You zoom past my father's plow
And zip around the Jersey cow.
The barley has no flowers for you;
You're headed to the flowers blue.

Here within the abbey wall,
It's like a little flower ball.
The bluebells dance in the breeze
And welcome all the honey bees.

One hundred flowers on your trip,
But now the rain starts to drip.
So it's time you're headed back
With pollen in your little sac.

The turkey and the donkey
Watch you stop upon the parsley
For one last sip before you dive
Into your safe honey hive.

BOOK
8

MOSS

Soft C and G

The Good and the Beautiful

There is a good chance you'll find some moss
in any forest you visit, but some forests have
an abundance of moss.

Most plants grow in soil, but moss has no roots and can grow on many surfaces: trees, rocks, bricks, concrete, on top of water, under water, and more.

Moss is found on every continent. Mosses like moist, shady places, so most do not grow well in deserts.

Moss can be an excellent choice to enhance a garden because moss needs little care and can provide beauty. You might notice birds using moss as a soft lining for their nests. However, moss can damage a roof.

Moss holds water like a sponge. Gardeners are urged to add moss to their soil because it helps the soil retain water.

In cold places, certain animals eat moss, such as arctic hares, bison, lemmings, geese, voles, and musk oxen.

BOOK 9

FOREST ELEPHANTS

PH; TCH

The Good AND THE Beautiful

African forest elephants usually spend their whole lives with their herds, but this elephant just became an orphan when its mother died.

Without its mother's milk, the elephant would die within a few days. Blessedly, it is found and taken to an elephant orphanage. Here the elephant is watched over twenty-four hours a day. The person taking care of the elephant sleeps by it and feeds it milk every few hours.

The people at the orphanage know that elephants need to play and be loved. The elephant stretches on the ball while Ralph creates a graph to track the elephant's growth. Ralph is not there every day. The workers switch around so the elephant does not get too attached to a single person.

The elephant has been at the orphanage for two years now and is getting bigger. It learns things elephants do. It has an itch, so it rubs and scratches its back against the tree bark.

Joseph starts feeding the elephant things other than milk. Does it eat gophers or dolphins? No! It eats plants, bark, and fruit. Today it eats a patch of grass and carrots.

Finally, after four years, the elephant is ready to take care of itself, and it is brought back to the wild. Joseph and Ralph take photos as the elephant plods off with its herd.

BOOK
10

HUMMINGBIRDS

O Can Say the Short U Sound

The Good and the Beautiful

Illustrated by Denise Hughes

goodandbeautiful.com

Sophia and her son Ace love hummingbirds so much that they keep a hummingbird book. It contains a ton of facts and notes about things they discover as they observe hummingbirds. Among the hummingbirds that come to their backyard feeder is the black-chinned hummingbird.

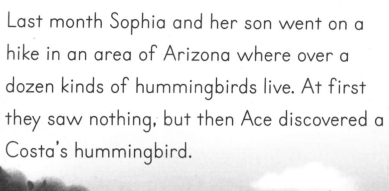

Last month Sophia and her son went on a hike in an area of Arizona where over a dozen kinds of hummingbirds live. At first they saw nothing, but then Ace discovered a Costa's hummingbird.

Sophia wrote notes in their book. Ace watched in wonder as the hummingbird hovered in place, beating its wings so fast the wings were just a blur.

An hour later, they spotted a ruby-throated hummingbird. Male and female ruby-throated hummingbirds are different colors. This male has an emerald-green back and a ruby-red throat in the front.

Sophia told her son that hummingbirds can see colors very well. This kind of hummingbird prefers orange and red flowers.

The last hummingbird they observed on their hike was a blue-throated hummingbird. "This wonderful bird," said Sophia, "has a long tongue that it sticks in and out of the flower several times per second, lapping up the nectar."

BOOK 11

ORCHARDS

UI and UE

The Good and the Beautiful

An orchard is a place where fruit or nut trees grow. Certain areas of the world are suited for certain kinds of fruits and nuts.

For example, apples grow well in places with cold winters and cool summers.

Olive trees need long, hot summers and winters that don't get too cold.

Fruits and nuts from the orchards of the world are sold whole or dried or are pressed into juice or liquids, like oil or nut milk.

Almond trees truly love California's hot and sunny summers. The majority of the world's almonds are grown there. Pollinating California's almond orchards is a huge and

unique event. Over one million beehives are trucked into the area, and billions of bees buzz around the pink and white blossoms.

Do you know what kind of orchard this is? Here is a clue: the fruit has a purple or reddish hue. Birds are not welcome guests because they ruin the fruit. It's a plum orchard!

This year the orchard owner hired a falconer to bring his falcon so that it could cruise across the orchard and pursue the other birds. It worked—the birds stayed away.

A pear orchard bursting with white blossoms is an incredible sight. There are over three thousand kinds of pears.

Pears bruise easily and are mushy if they ripen on the tree, so they are picked before they are fully ripe.

Orchards are wonderful blessings that bring great value and beauty to our world.

BOOK
12

DROUGHT

Sight Words: Group 2

The Good and the Beautiful

A drought is when a certain area gets less than its normal amount of rain over an extended period of time. This is how an area of California looked before a drought. It was so pleasant and lush.

This is how the same area looks after years of drought. Along the whole length of the lake, everything is brown and dry, and the water is so low. I bend down and touch the cracked, dry earth.

It hasn't rained for many months. Oh, how we need rain! The farmers' crops are drooping and dying, and everywhere water is scarce.

One day, I grab a book from a drawer by our piano. I sit in the armchair and read. I hear a curious sound and stop reading. I listen hard. *Plop! Pitter! Patter!*

I run to the window and look out. Rain! It starts to come faster and faster until it is like a fountain spraying over the land. I cheer! If we keep getting rain in the weeks and months ahead, our drought will get better and go away one day.

LAMB'S FIRST DAY

MB; DGE

The
Good AND THE Beautiful

Illustrated by McKenzie West

goodandbeautiful.com

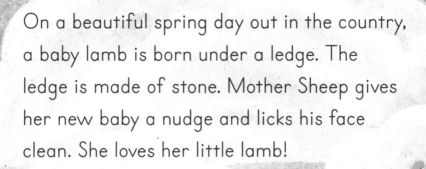

On a beautiful spring day out in the country, a baby lamb is born under a ledge. The ledge is made of stone. Mother Sheep gives her new baby a nudge and licks his face clean. She loves her little lamb!

The farmer combs his fingers through the lamb's soft wool. He gives the mother sheep some porridge to eat. Mother Sheep is hungry, but the lamb just wants to play in the tulips.

The curious lamb explores the
area. He sees a partridge with a red beak
on a tree limb. He sees a badger with white
stripes by the ridge. He sees ants climb on the
fence, one by one. What a beautiful day!

Today the baby lamb will join the flock. The farmer snaps his finger and thumb, and Mother Sheep starts to walk. Baby Lamb runs across the bridge and down the hill. There are so many sheep here!

The sheep walk down to the edge of the
river. They dodge trees and stay in a group.
Baby Lamb starts to fidget. He wants to run
and jump. The other lambs want to play, too.

It has been a long day. Baby Lamb and Mother Sheep trudge home. They climb under the ledge and snuggle down to sleep. What a beautiful first day for Baby Lamb!

THE PLANETS

EIGH

The Good and the Beautiful

The sun is an important source of energy. It takes light from the sun eight minutes to reach Earth, even though they are millions of miles apart. The sun weighs more than all the planets combined! There are eight planets orbiting the sun.

The planet nearest to the sun is Mercury. It is the smallest planet. Eighteen planets the size of Mercury could fit inside our earth. Mercury is rocky and has no moons, and a year on Mercury lasts only eighty-eight days!

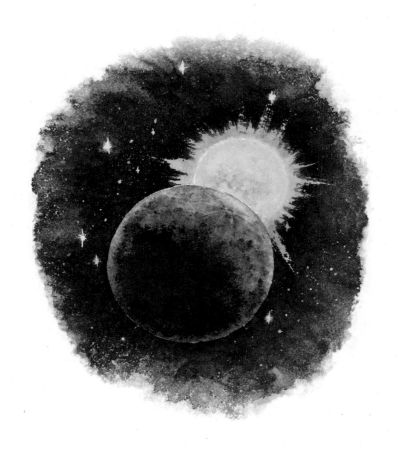

Mercury's closest neighbor is Venus. Venus is the hottest planet. On Venus the sun rises in the west and sets in the east. A one-hundred-pound person on Earth would weigh only ninety-one pounds on Venus.

The third planet is our own beautiful Earth. Then comes our red neighbor, Mars. Mars has two moons and is a cold, icy world. Its red color comes from a kind of metal in the dirt. The tallest mountain on any of the planets is found here; it is two-and-a-half times the height of Mt. Everest.

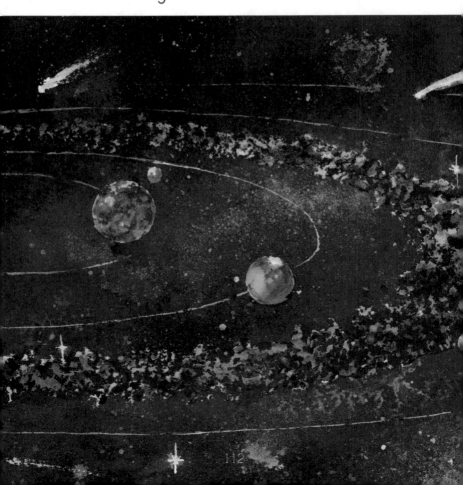

The fifth planet is Jupiter. It is the biggest planet but does not have solid land. It is made out of gas! Jupiter has almost eighty moons! Next you will find Saturn with its rings of ice and rock. Saturn weighs as much as ninety-five Earths put together.

The seventh planet is Uranus, which is a beautiful blue color due to a gas called methane. It is the only planet that spins on its side. Its neighbor is Neptune, the eighth and final planet. Uranus and Neptune are both called "ice giants." Because they are so far from the sun, they are always cold.

BOOK 15

VOLCANOES

IE

The Good and the Beautiful

A volcano is a crack in the earth's surface. These cracks are often found in mountains like this one and can be found on land and under the ocean, too! The world's largest volcano that still erupts is in Hawaii. Many movies have been filmed there.

There are two main types of volcanoes. The volcano in this field is cone shaped with steep slopes. It achieves this shape as thick lava flows down the sides and then cools and becomes hard.

This volcano is called a shield volcano. It is wider, and the sides are not as steep as the ones on a cone-shaped volcano. The lava from shield volcanoes is thin and runny. It flows farther down the mountain before it cools.

Did you know that magma and lava are not the same thing? Magma is the name for matter that is inside the volcano, and lava is what we call that material once it comes out of the volcano.

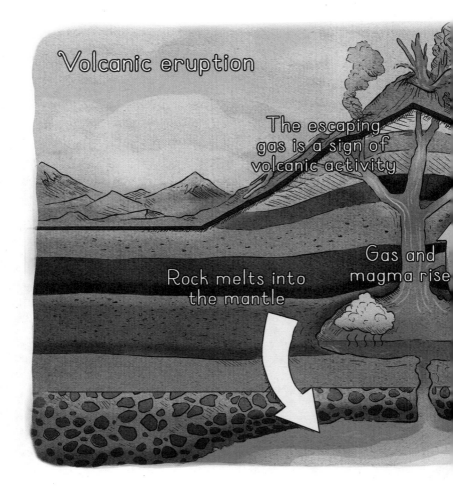

Volcanic eruption

The escaping gas is a sign of volcanic activity

Rock melts into the mantle

Gas and magma rise

Magma is made up of melted rock, pieces of solid rock, and gas. Magma is hotter than lava, which cools as it leaves the volcano. Magma sits in the magma chamber inside the volcano until it erupts.

Eruption releases lava down the side of the volcano

Lava cools and becomes rock

Magma rises up to the chamber

The opening of a volcano is called the crater. People who study volcanoes can spend only a brief time at the crater. It is very hot up there! They check the heat levels and retrieve samples to study. They wear masks or tie scarves around their faces to keep out the ash.

How do we know when a volcano is going to erupt? More gas comes out of the volcano than normal. It might also grumble or shriek or even make the earth shake. The crater may change shape or height as the magma under it starts to move.

Volcanoes are beautiful but can also be scary. It is a relief to know that most people will never see a volcano erupt in person. And people who live near volcanoes have learned how to take care when the lava starts to flow.

Pacific Ring of Fire

BOOK
16

THE STORM

OUR and OUGH

The Good and the Beautiful

Illustrated by Larissa Sharina

goodandbeautiful.com

The day was bright; the sky was clear.
The sun was warm enough.
Then the gray clouds crowded near,
And the skies got dark and rough.

The winds blew in; the leaves blew down,
Their battle bravely fought.
In sweeps of red and gold and brown,
They are gone without a thought.

The rain came in with wet, cold drops.
The skies began to pour.
Rain fell on homes and kids and crops.
It fell on trees and more.

The thunder crashed; the lightning flashed.
The source was close and loud.
Who would have thought that such a noise
Could come from in a cloud?

The storm is big; the storm is tough.
It rains both far and wide.
The storm is loud; the storm is rough,
But we are safe inside.

Inside the house I'm safe and warm
While the storm blows through.
Why should I worry about the storm
When I am here with you!

THE SUN

Words with Silent Letters

The Good and the Beautiful

Illustrated by Alessia Turchie

The sun peeks up over the land and glistens
on the wet grass. It creates a subtle glow
as it slowly rises into the sky. The morning
scene is quiet and calm on this beautiful
island. The sun brings life to all it touches.

The sun rises in the east, no matter where
you are in the world. Sunrise is also called
dawn, daybreak, or first light. There is
never any doubt that the sun will come up
every morning in a column of light. Listen,
and you can hear the birds chirping to greet

the dawn. The rustle of the bushes tells us
that the deer and rabbits are awake, too.
Some flowers turn their faces toward the
rising sun and spread their beautiful scent.
In the spring and summer, the earth tilts
toward the sun, and the days are longer.

The sun sets in the west, no matter where you are in the world. Sunset is also called twilight, dusk, or nightfall. The light fades and softens as the sun nestles down into the mountains and trees. While you are getting ready for bed, some animals are just waking

up. The owls, raccoons, and foxes stretch
their muscles and hustle out to find food in
the dark. They move silently. In the winter
and autumn, the earth tilts away from the
sun, and the nights are longer.

When is the longest day? The answer depends on where you live. If you live in the northern half of the earth, the longest day of the year is in June. Parts of Alaska get twenty-two hours of daylight in the summer!

But if you live in the southern half of the earth, the longest day of the year is in December! In Australia it is hot and sunny for Christmas. The tilt of the earth makes the days longer or shorter as it circles the sun.

The sun is a gift from God. It rises and sets
every day in a dance like a beautiful ballet.
It makes life possible on our earth. Sunlight
helps plants, animals, and kids grow. We
honor God when we take care of the planet
He made.

SEAHORSE

TI Can Say /SH/

The Good and the Beautiful

Illustrated by Jennifer Falkner

© 2022 Jenny Phillips

goodandbeautiful.com

Look closely. Something is hiding in the seagrass. It's a seahorse! Can you find it? Seahorses are terrible swimmers, so hiding in the grass is a good solution to stay safe. They can even change the color of their bodies to match the grass around them.

Don't be fooled. A seahorse isn't a horse
at all. It's a fish! It uses gills to breathe
and has a tough, bony body. Seahorses are
the slowest fish, but they can move in all
directions in the water. They can swim
in a forward motion, but also backward,
upward, and downward.

A seahorse needs patience as it looks
for food. Seahorses have no teeth and no
stomachs, so they must eat a lot of small
food to stay alive. A seahorse can eat up to
three thousand pieces of food a day! One
option for dinner is small shrimp. Another is
plankton. Yum!

Every day, seahorse couples greet each other with an unusual action. They dance in a circle around each other. Seahorses have strong, flexible tails that can grab a section of seagrass or other plants. Seahorses often swim in pairs, with their tails linked together. Isn't that so cute?

Do you know what happens before baby seahorses are born? The female gives the eggs to the male, and he carries the eggs in his pouch until they are ready to be born. More than one thousand seahorse babies, called *fry*, can be born at one time. Only a small fraction of the babies will live to be adults.

Seahorses have very good eyesight. Each eye can move by itself, so a seahorse can look forward and backward at the same time! Without question the seahorse is a beautiful and curious creation of our God. Seahorses are wonderful additions to life in the deep blue seas.

BOOK
19

THE AMAZING POLAR BEAR

CI; GN, IGN, AUGH

In a land of ancient glaciers, a mother polar bear gave birth to two daughters. They began their lives in a den. It was made of snow and was not very spacious, but the mother designed the den as a refuge from wind and snow and to keep the cubs safe from predators.

The mother caught a bearded seal and shared it with her cubs. They thought it was a delicious meal! The mother bear has already taught her cubs how to swim, and eventually, she will teach them how to hunt.

At any sign of danger, the mother polar
bear will defend her precious young cubs
ferociously.

After three years, the cubs are grown and are ready to be on their own. Polar bears are not very social, so when they don't have cubs, they are by themselves. This polar bear is now on her own.

She is made especially for extremely cold weather. Under her fur, a layer of blubber that is four inches thick is crucial to keeping her warm. She also has fur on the bottoms of her feet.

God designed polar bears with large webbed forepaws that allow them to swim long distances. They can swim for hours, and they can hold their breath underwater for two minutes. Polar bears have longer necks than other kinds of bears, and this allows them to keep their heads above water when swimming.

BOOK 20

WINTER SNOW

Sight Words: Group 3

The Good and the Beautiful

Every year in the fall, snow comes to my mountain. While the brightly colored leaves dance in the valley, the flakes begin to fly up on the mountain. The tall peaks are dusted with white, like a cake is dusted with sugar. That's how I know winter is on the way.

Soon the snow creeps down the mountain and into my valley. Now there is laughter and fun as we play in the cold. The fluffy, wet snow cushions our falls as we sled down the hills. The cold air and sunny skies brighten my soul.

The men hitch up the horses and journey into the forest. They cut the wood we need to fuel our winter fires. The women make soup and cocoa to warm them up and laugh at the snowmen the children make.

When I go outside, I must wear my warm clothes. That is the rule. I pull on my warm socks and then my boots. I wear a sweater, a coat, a scarf, and a pointed hat that my mother made. I wear so many clothes I can barely move!

The winter days grow short and dark. The sun goes to bed so early, and the night wind is cruel and cold. Around the fireplace, Father tells a story while he carves a little wooden horse. Mother sews a cushion and hands out warm food.

Then one bright day, the snow in the valley melts away, and the green grass appears. The happy flowers show their faces, and the birds begin to call. I watch the snow creep back up the mountain to the very top. That's how I know that spring is on the way.

Book
21

VENUS FLYTRAP

EI; AL

The
Good AND THE Beautiful

Deep inside the cool, damp forest grows a small plant. Among the pine trees and the vines and the mosses, you can find it. It grows close to the ground, in small groups. Its beautiful red or pink color makes it look like a flower, but don't let that deceive you. This weird plant has a special ability for survival.

It waits, still and quiet, in the soft sunshine for the arrival of its favorite food. After a few hours, it finally senses something; a small beetle is crawling across its sharp, green hairs. *Whoosh!* Quick as a blink, the plant closes its trap to seize the beetle. The Venus flytrap has caught its dinner.

Most plants make their own food from the sun. But some plants need more food and protein than they receive from just sunshine. In general, Venus flytraps will eat ants, beetles, spiders, and other insects. It can take around ten days for a plant to eat one insect.

Venus flytraps grow best in mild locations, near tropical areas. They are native to North and South Carolina in the United States. Venus flytraps are not the only meat-eating plants in the world, but they reign as the most popular. They make good personal houseplants.

Venus flytraps are smart plants. They know not to close their traps for things like raindrops or wind. If a Venus flytrap does accidentally close on something it can't eat, it can spit out that object from its trap. Each Venus flytrap produces white flowers with green veins every year to create new plants.

All Venus flytraps have a seasonal time where they are dormant. That means they need to rest. They grow and bloom in the spring and summer and then rest in the fall and winter. Venus flytraps seem to be animals or machines, but they are neither. They are special plants with incredible skills.

PYGMY OWL

CH Can Say /K/;
Y in the Middle of a Word

Illustrated by Yana Zybina

goodandbeautiful.com